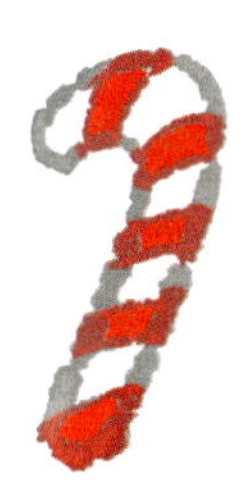

MW01629010

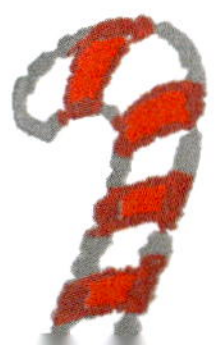

For YOU and ME!

Winter is...
Rhyme in Time Series

barbarapinke.com

First edition 2024

ISBN 978-3-949736-79-7 (paperback)
ISBN 978-3-949736-80-3 (hardcover)
ISBN 978-3-949736-81-0 (e-book)

Written by Barbara Pinke
Edited by Andrea Ketchelmeier
Illustrated by Alvin Adhi
Designed by Gábor Dinya

Publisher's Cataloging-in-Publication Data
Names: Pinke, Barbara, author. | Adhi, Alvin, illustrator.
Title: Winter is... / written by Barbara Pinke; illustrated by Alvin Adhi.
Series: Rhyme in Time
Description: Barbara Pinke, 2024. | Summary: This book celebrates the magic of winter, highlighting frosty days, swirling snowflakes, evergreen trees, and cozy treats. This short rhyming story takes readers on a heartwarming journey through the season's sparkling beauty and joyful wonders.
Identifiers: ISBN: 978-3-949-736-80-3 (hardcover) | 978-3-949-736-79-7 (paperback) | 978-3-949-736-81-0 (ebook)
Subjects: LCSH Winter--Juvenile fiction. | Snow--Juvenile fiction. | Seasons--Juvenile fiction. | Stories in verse. | BISAC JUVENILE FICTION / Concepts / Seasons | JUVENILE FICTION / Stories in Verse
Classification: LCC PZ7.1 .P56 Wi 2024 | DDC [E]--dc23

Written by
Barbara Pinke

Illustrated by
Alvin Adhi

I have a poster on my wall
of winter, summer, spring, and fall.

Cold or warm or leafless tree,
every season's great to me.

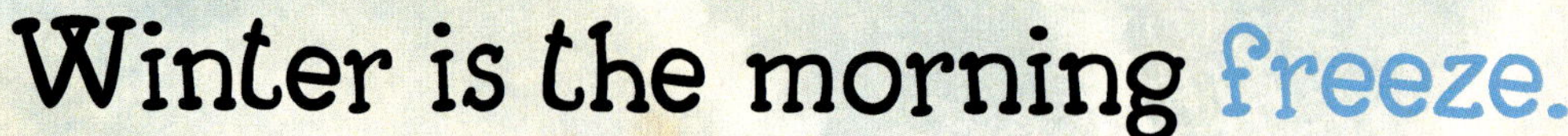

Winter is the morning freeze.

Winter is the resting bees.

Winter is the ginger tea.

Winter is the stormy sea.

Winter is the falling snow.

Winter is the candle's glow.

Winter is the woolen hat.

Winter is the purring cat.

Winter is a snowball fight.

Winter is the longest night.

Winter is the woodpecker's drums.

Winter is the gingerbread crumbs.

Winter is the cozy bed.

Winter is the cheeks so red.

Winter is the sleeping bear.

Winter is the rocking chair.

Winter is the steaming mugs.

Winter is for warm, tight hugs.

Winter is for movie time.

Winter is for grandma's rhyme.

Winter is the snowman's grin.

Winter is where
dreams begin.

ABOUT THE ILLUSTRATOR

Alvin Adhi is an illustrator who loves nature.
He loves to draw living things with any emotion that is contained in them.

Alvin is also an observer. Every shape, texture, and color fascinates him, such as the beauty of snowflakes that are variegated and perfectly shaped. The laughter of children playing in the snow and the sound of music on the streets make him happy in winter.

Besides drawing, he likes gardening and fishkeeping.
He hopes that through his art, he can put a smile on your face.

Email: alvintheillustrator@gmail.com
Facebook: @alvinadhi
Instagram: @alvin_adhi

ABOUT THE AUTHOR

Barbara Pinke is a multi-award-winning author who loves to create stories and spice them up with adventure and fun.

She was born and raised in Hungary and later hopscotched across Europe before settling in Germany.

Website: barbarapinke.com
Email: barbara@barbarapinke.com
Facebook and Instagram: @barbarapinke.author

OTHER BOOKS BY THE AUTHOR

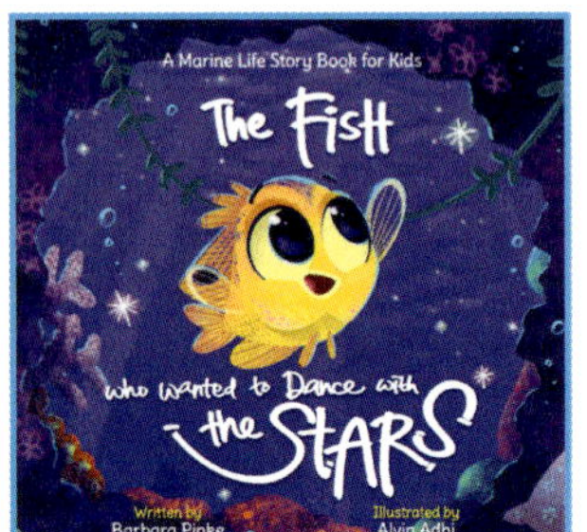

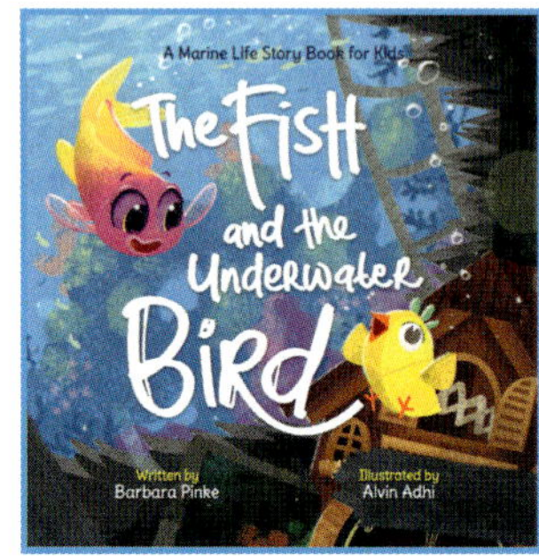

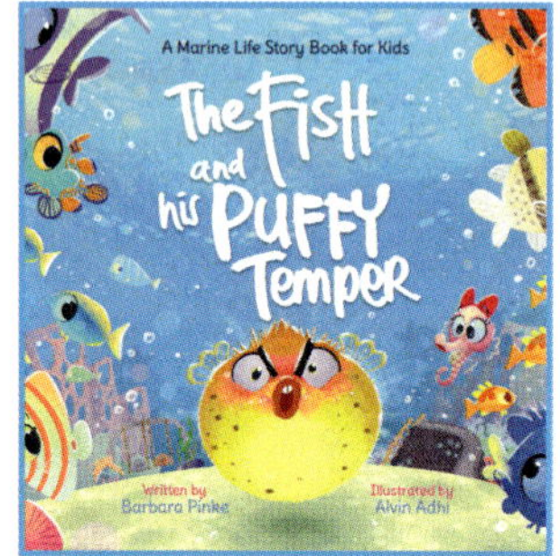

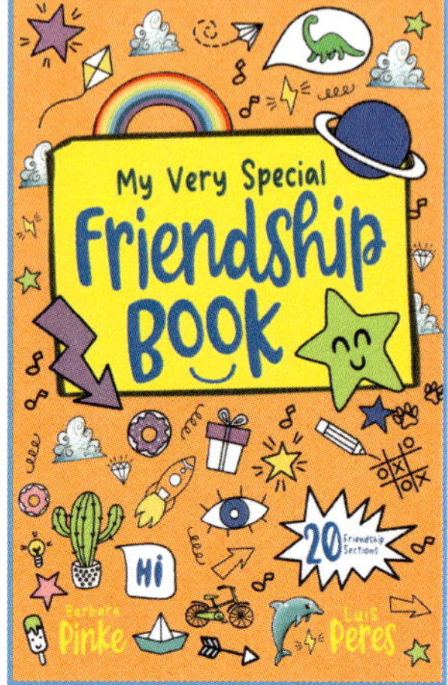

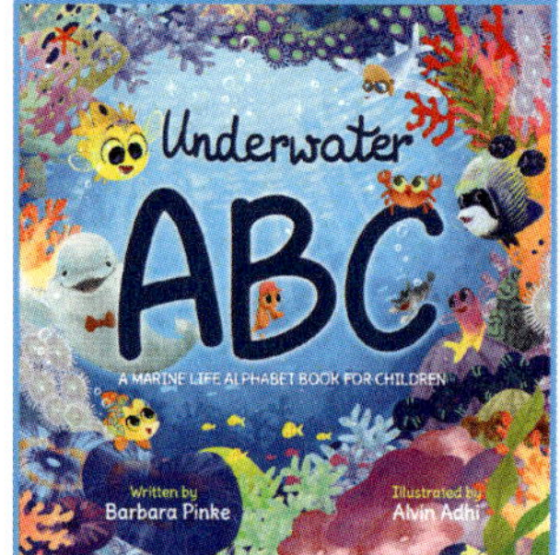

GET IN TOUCH

Scan this QR code to go to barbarapinke.com where you can find information about other adventures and a dedicated space, FunZone. Get your freebies: mazes, word searches, coloring sheets, and more.

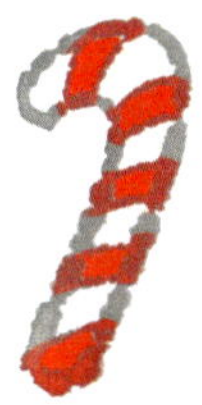

I hope you have enjoyed my story. Your feedback is very important to me, and I would love to hear your thoughts on my work. If you have a few moments, please consider leaving a review online. Your review will not only help me improve my content, but also help others who are looking for similar information.

Thank you in advance for your time and support!

 barbarapinke.com

 barbara@barbarapinke.com

   @barbarapinke.author

  @barbarapinkeauthor

You can also follow me on BookBub and Goodreads.

Made in the USA
Middletown, DE
09 January 2026

26794283R00018